How to Homeschool Independently

Do-it-Yourself Secrets to
Rekindle the
Love of Learning

Lee Binz,
The HomeScholar

© 2015 by **The HomeScholar LLC**

All Rights Reserved. No part of this publication may be reproduced in any form or by any means, including scanning, photocopying, or otherwise without prior written permission of the copyright holder.

First Printing, 2015

Printed in the United States of America

ISBN: 1515080129
ISBN-13: 978-1515080121

Disclaimer: Parents assume full responsibility for the education of their children in accordance with state law. College requirements vary, so make sure to check with the colleges about specific requirements for homeschoolers. We offer no guarantees, written or implied, that the use of our products and services will result in college admissions or scholarship awards.

How to Homeschool Independently

Do-it-Yourself Secrets to
Rekindle the
Love of Learning

What are Coffee Break Books?

How to Homeschool Independently is part of The HomeScholar's Coffee Break Book series.

Designed especially for parents who don't want to spend hours and hours reading a 400-page book on homeschooling high school, each book combines Lee's practical and friendly approach with detailed, but easy-to-digest information, perfect to read over a cup of coffee at your favorite coffee shop!

Never overwhelming, always accessible and manageable, each book in the series will give parents the tools they need to tackle the tasks of homeschooling high school, one warm sip at a time.

Everything about these Coffee Break Books is designed to suggest simplicity, ease and comfort - from the size (fits in a purse), to the font and paragraph length (easy on the eyes), to the price (the same as a Starbucks Venti Triple Caramel Macchiato). Unlike a fancy coffee drink, however, these books are guilt-free pleasures you will want to enjoy again and again!

Table of Contents

What are Coffee Break Books? v
Declare Your Homeschool Independence 9
Homeschooling Outside the Box! 19
Common Questions 29
Requirements for Success 41
Problems with Dependence 49
Systemic Educational Problems 65
First Steps Toward Independence 71
Plan Classes and Choose Resources 79
Avoid Fads and Pitfalls 87
How to Teach the Hard Stuff 91
Homeschooling is Your Job! 97
Taking Charge 101
Who is Lee Binz and What Can She Do for Me? 105
Testimonials 107
Also From The HomeScholar... 111

Chapter 1

Declare Your Homeschool Independence

Celebrate your inalienable right to homeschool your way! Keep life, liberty and the pursuit of happiness at the center of your homeschool! Parents who start homeschooling independently often feel like they're getting their life back. Instead of being powerless while their children are indoctrinated by the state in a public school, they finally have the freedom to teach their children consistent with their own values. Parents often feel they have the time to pursue happiness while homeschooling, instead of pursuing the busyness so common in our society.

Sign Your Declaration of Independence

In many states, the first way to declare your independence is to sign a declaration indicating your intent to homeschool. If it is required by your state, make sure you complete the declaration of independence. By signing, you declare the school is no longer responsible for your child's education; you are responsible for your child's education. Know your state homeschool law and read it carefully. You can learn about your state's homeschool law here:

http://www.thehomescholar.com/know-your-state-homeschool-law.php.

Be a fearless leader and declare your independence from the public school system. Skip the public school requirements, which are so arbitrary and ever changing, and stick to your state homeschool law. Create your own declaration of independence; withdraw from the public system and rigid classroom structure, so your child's education can be a perfect fit.

Tell people about your decision to homeschool. You may want to explain to them what homeschooling means, if they aren't familiar with it. Notify your family, inform and explain if you would like to, but don't rationalize your decision or ask for permission. This is a decision made by you, the child's parents, not by committee. You may express a patient, loving attitude, by simply saying, "I appreciate your concern, but I am responsible for my child's education."

Embrace the Homeschool Lifestyle

Homeschooling doesn't end with declaring your independence – it's the beginning of your homeschool life and responsibilities. Our founding fathers successfully declared independence because they seized the responsibility of governing. Be like the founding fathers! Seize the responsibility of homeschooling. Minimize delegation, and resist enrolling, registering, or enlisting in a program. The homeschool lifestyle is at home, shaping and molding your children in your day-to-day interactions. If you aren't home, it becomes more difficult to embrace the lifestyle of learning that enables homeschooling to be more fruitful.

Watch for natural learning. Learning isn't limited to a specific time or place, it's integrated into life. It is not boxed in by a school year, between the hours of 9:00 am and 3:00 pm daily. The homeschool life is REAL life, not a make-believe world of age-segregated groups. Embrace the freedom to learn naturally. Go textbook-free and focus on real-life learning, apart from grade-level workbooks and dry textbooks with limited information.

Educate with Liberty

Embrace your freedom and go classroom free. When you avoid a school mentality and grade-level thinking, you can truly educate with liberty. Your children will never need to be labeled "below grade-level" again, and you will begin to recognize that learning is the key, not standardized tests. You can educate at the perfect pace for your child, learning on purpose every day.

You are homeschooling in freedom but homeschooling independently does not mean going it alone. You're not alone – you have your spouse, your children, and your support group. Millions of people homeschool; the numbers are constantly growing as people flee public education. People have homeschooled for many years. You have the freedom you need to educate your children in a way that makes sense for them.

With the freedom to educate in a meaningful way, you can choose curriculum that fits your child's learning style and interests. Interested and engaged children learn more. The freedom to engage in unusual learning opportunities can help your children identify their passions, which can help them decide on their college and career goals. Learning in freedom will create leaders of tomorrow who are passionate about improving life, liberty, and the pursuit of happiness for others.

Pursue a Relaxed, Fun, Educational Experience

Happiness isn't a pie-in-the-sky wish; it's a key ingredient for learning. The safe, secure, fun, and free atmosphere of learning at home is a better way to educate children of all ages. Be sure to discover your children's learning styles, and be mindful of your own learning style. Education at home is faster, more convenient and more efficient. It doesn't require tests. It's less stressful, takes less time, and allows more time for fun. When you embrace learning with reckless abandon, your children can wiggle as much as they need to, follow along with audiobooks until they are 18, or solve medical mysteries when they are teenagers; it's all part of their homeschool education.

Encourage delight directed learning. While we want our children to be well educated, and we have to cover core subjects, we can still manage to pursue happiness. Everyone has subjects they don't enjoy, but parents can make the drudgery of a subject more fun with games and meaningful experiences. Everyone has a subject they love, whether it's math, music, writing, or P.E. Public education has the ball and chain of common core classes and electives are limited to classes teachers are interested in. When you homeschool, you can create an elective out of almost any of your student's interests. Center core classes on your child's learning style, to maximize their delight in learning and help them develop to their maximum potential.

Celebrate Independence

Celebrate your independence responsibly. Make sure you are in control, not someone else. Keep a firm grip on the benefits of homeschooling independently and allow your children to learn with reckless abandon. You don't need to be a certified teacher or have college credentials to homeschool your children. Teachers learn to teach groups and manage a classroom. While these are valuable classroom skills, they are not necessary in your homeschool. Don't let anyone make you feel afraid of college, scholarships, transcript, diploma, or career preparation – the average parent is completely capable of homeschooling children successfully into adulthood.

While you revel in your freedom, don't forget the prime directive: education. You could get lost in your freedom and spend years in your pajamas in front of a flashing screen, but freedom means responsibility. You don't want to produce feral children, like cats left free to forage on their own. You don't want to produce moral, faithful, but illiterate children who love the Lord but can't spell to save their lives. Educate on purpose while parenting your children, so you can shape and mold their heart and soul as they grow.

Chill Out

Relax! Homeschooling is fun! You're not jumping out of the frying pan into the fire. Homeschooling is a real, legitimate, no-more-tears formula for educating children. Children should learn at their own pace. Keep moving forward in your plan to educate your kids. Make sure each subject is challenging, but not overwhelming, so your kids can enjoy learning. As you shape and mold your children's character and behavior, it becomes easier to enjoy homeschooling. Grab some iced tea or lemonade and put your feet up. Relax! Homeschooling is going to be fun!

Independence Checklist

1. Check your state homeschool law
2. Locate support
3. Determine your interim plan
4. Get to know your child
5. Learn more about homeschooling
6. Plan your subjects
7. Choose your resources
8. Purchase materials
9. Learn on purpose every day
10. Keep calm and homeschool on

Lee Binz, The HomeScholar

Chapter 2

Homeschooling Outside the Box!

Brick and mortar schools box children in. Children are forced into a one-size-fits-all container. Usually schools gear learning towards the middle 20%, which means approximately 80% of children will not fit inside the box. In schools, all children use the same curriculum and take the same tests. Homeschooling allows children to step outside the box; they can stretch out when they're ready. In the homeschool, kids never have to feel as if the box is so big for them that they're behind, or so small it restricts them from advancing.

For many children, school can be like forcing a square peg into a round hole. A wiggly kid with ADHD doesn't do well sitting still in a desk for eight hours a day. My own child could do advanced math for his age when he was in kindergarten. He didn't fit in the school environment because he wasn't allowed to work to his ability. Homeschooling independently is always a good fit for your child. You can consider the needs of your child and can fit the education to their needs.

Finding Their Fit

> "Everybody is a genius. But if you judge a fish by its ability to climb a tree, it will live its whole life believing that it is stupid."
> ~ Albert Einstein

A child may have dyslexia, and because of their inability to read at grade level, spend their school years believing they're stupid. It can take entering the working world before they recognize the gifts that the public education system didn't recognize and that they are, in fact, quite capable.

One of my clients is starting to homeschool her ninth grader, a high-functioning autistic child. She has the power to ensure her child graduates with meaningful classes. Her child has the potential to go on to college and career well prepared, instead of feeling incompetent or like they couldn't measure up or didn't fit in.

Freedom and Responsibility

Homeschooling independently means freedom, but freedom comes with great responsibility. You can look to the scriptures for guidance.

> "All things are lawful, but not all things are helpful. All things are lawful, but not all things build up." 1 Corinthians 10:23

Not all of the opportunities and learning activities available to you are going to benefit your child. If you do too much, you will burn out. Don't go to excess. Even though you have unlimited options when you homeschool independently, not everything will build up or edify your child.

Learning with Reckless Abandon

> "For freedom Christ has set us free; stand firm therefore and do not submit again to a yoke of slavery." Galatians 5:1

Sometimes that's how it feels when you start homeschooling for the first time. It's as if you are throwing off the yoke of slavery of being part of the public school system. You can start thinking outside the box!

Independent homeschooling can mean learning with reckless abandon. You can have fun! There are unlimited options. You can make sure each class you teach is challenging for your child but not overwhelming. Challenging but not overwhelming is a good description of the perfect job and the same holds true of homeschooling. The academics you provide can always be challenging even if your child is gifted, but never need to be overwhelming even if your child is below grade level.

Real World Preparation

Homeschooling through high school is a wonderful way to prepare children for a real world job. You can make sure your homeschool courses are challenging by teaching every subject at your student's ability level, even if it changes from subject to subject. You don't have to worry about the math level you think they should be in; you can focus on what they are capable of now and work on keeping them challenged.

We have the power to use methods and a curriculum that works or to choose an alternative when it isn't working. As homeschoolers, we can meet our children's specific learning styles. By doing so, we can ensure our children enjoy learning.

Homeschooling independently also provides socialization that reflects the real world. Kids can interact with people of all ages and backgrounds instead of sitting in a classroom, inside the box, surrounded by kids the exact same age eight hours a day. In the working world, people aren't restricted to working with only their age mates. Homeschooling is more like the real world.

Safe and Secure

Children can learn in the safety and security of your own home, where they learn best. Feeling safe and secure can improve your child's learning success. Safety and security is a huge hurdle for public and private schools to overcome because of violence and bullying inherent in schools.

When people ask, "What does homeschooling look like?" I usually talk about what it looked like in my home; it looked like my son lying on top of our dog reading a book, or talking to his grandfather about economics. This is an environment free of fear, where children have the security to learn with reckless abandon.

In a public high school, electives are often chosen according to the teacher's interests. When you homeschool, the sky's the limit; you can choose electives based on your children's interests. These interests can help them to prepare for college and career. Specialization means allowing children to pursue their own interests.

Homeschoolers also have more free time. It doesn't always feel that way because we're still busy, but our children don't have to spend hours standing in line, riding the school bus, or finishing homework. Homeschooling gives children the time to pursue meaningful activities and interests of their own.

What Parents Can't Do

There are some limits to our responsibilities as parents. The truth is, even the best homeschooling parents cannot make children learn – learning is the child's responsibility. Your responsibility is simply to provide the opportunity for them to learn in a challenging but not overwhelming way.

Accept that you can't force your children to learn.

You also can't change your children. They have unique traits and characteristics; you can't force them to become someone they're not. You can't force a child who is wiggly with ADHD to sit still as if they're chained to the desk. God makes each child unique. You can't change your child's learning styles and innate abilities.

One reason public schools are failing children is they can't change them or make them learn. That certainly doesn't stop schools from trying, however! They put 30 kids behind desks and make them all learn the same way, at the same rate, using the same curriculum.

Public schools are losing children to boredom. The dropout rate is staggering in some parts of the country. Think about your child's learning style, innate abilities, and your goals and priorities for them. Homeschooling can be effective. You can adapt on the fly as conditions change, instead of sticking to a public school's inflexible curriculum.

You also can't force children to make wise decisions. My husband and I found that out ourselves. I wish homeschooling could guarantee your children will always make good choices. It doesn't work that way because each individual has free will. A home education cannot compel your child to share your views. You can't force children to adopt excellent character qualities or to share your personal values.

At the same time, your children will be surrounded by your faith, character, and values on a day-to-day basis, and are more likely to retain those values as adults. You can't make them choose wisely all the time. Your homeschool goals can only cover what you can control. You can only control your own behavior; you can't control your children's behavior.

Chapter 3

Common Questions

There are common questions everyone has about homeschooling, especially independent homeschooling. If you have already begun to homeschool, you've probably heard some of these questions already.

1. What about socialization?

This is the number one question people ask about homeschooling. As a result, homeschoolers call socialization the "dreaded S word." New homeschoolers are surprised to find out that socialization is not a concern.

When we started homeschooling, I immediately noticed a dramatic improvement in my children's social skills. One of my sons was outgoing and a bit of a bully in public school. When we started homeschooling, he stopped bullying. My other son is introverted and shy; he became more outgoing and developed true friendships over time because he wasn't picked on in our homeschool.

Homeschoolers are better prepared for life because of socialization in the real world. Instead of spending eight hours a day with their same-age peers, homeschoolers have the opportunity to interact with a broad range of people, in a wide variety of different settings. This real world socialization leads to opportunities students in public school don't have.

My children each won a full-tuition scholarship competition from their first choice university. While they excelled academically in high school, we found out they won not because of their academics, nor because of their individual passionate pursuits of chess and economics; they won based on socialization. Since all the kids competing for scholarships had excellent academics and great personal stories, the college admissions staff told us they judged the kids largely based on how they interacted with other students and adults when they thought nobody was looking.

Colleges want students who are honest and trustworthy, who can hold a conversation with anybody of any age, and who can look people in the eye when talking. Homeschooling gives us the time to cultivate these excellent social skills.

2. What about college?

Homeschooling high school is becoming more common, and colleges are familiar with it. Colleges even try to attract homeschoolers through marketing campaigns and attending homeschool conventions. They want homeschoolers to attend their schools. Colleges love homeschoolers!

Homeschooling high school is great college preparation. By focusing on the content of education, instead of all of the time-wasting activities that occupy public school students, homeschoolers can learn more and learn more quickly. Parents can use the extra time to their benefit, by helping children dig deeper. It is not unusual for homeschool students to show an adult level of expertise in their areas of interest by the time they reach high school. One of my sons had a deep interest in economics and public policy, and the flexibility of homeschooling permitted him to intern at a public policy think tank starting when he was only 14 years old.

Developing unique pursuits like this is not unusual for homeschoolers. Perhaps you've noticed how homeschoolers dominate geography and spelling bees. This isn't because parents "pushed" them, but simply because of the profound independence allowed by their parents. The ability to "go deep" and "go wide" when studying their interests offers them a remarkable advantage over other students. It offers them the elusive ingredient that all colleges look for in their applicants — individuality. Independent homeschooling can give your children a real advantage when applying for college.

3. What about scholarships?

My children were both invited to compete for full-tuition scholarships. It was a full day competition at a Christian college, lasting eight hours. My shy child found it challenging to talk about himself and my outgoing child found it difficult not to dominate the conversation. My two boys won two of the ten four-year full-tuition scholarships the college offered that year, even though they have completely different personalities.

Your child can earn big scholarships, too. The best way to ensure your child will earn college scholarships is to plan a rigorous homeschool high school curriculum. There are certain minimum requirements colleges want to see in applicants, but if you want your child to win big scholarships, your student will need to exceed those requirements.

Another way to stand out from the crowd is to achieve good scores on the SAT or ACT. Colleges are ranked using their students' SAT and ACT scores. If the students' scores go up, the college receives a higher rating. Colleges pursue and reward students who will contribute to higher ratings.

Any student who demonstrates a special talent or passion will also stand out from the cookie-cutter kids colleges see all the time. Since homeschoolers have more time to specialize, this puts them at an advantage when applying for scholarships.

Private companies also offer scholarships. Merit based scholarships are won based on a student's accomplishments. For example, there are scholarships available for students who do volunteer work or participate in the Civil Air Patrol. A student can also apply for merit scholarships based on a special talent or ability, or based on their excellent academic record. These are just a few ways your student can earn BIG scholarships, and make attendance at the school of their dreams a reality!

4. Where do you get the curriculum?

The public school system doesn't hand you a curriculum when you start homeschooling. You can buy any curriculum you choose, from anywhere you want. That's the beauty of homeschooling independently! There are many options. You can find a curriculum online, at your local homeschool curriculum store, at a homeschool convention (new or used), or at the library.

Pick a curriculum that fits yours and your child's needs. I chose the Sonlight curriculum because I wanted something that would hold my hand through my first year of homeschooling independently. It's literature-based so it's great for kids who love to read.

There are many other types of homeschool curriculum, including Charlotte Mason, Classical, Thomas Jefferson, Waldorf, and Montessori. You can also go curriculum-free and choose unschooling. Don't jump right into anything, though. Read up on the different homeschool methods and decide what will work best for your family.

Don't worry about choosing the perfect curriculum; it doesn't exist. Any curriculum can help you get the job done. However, if you end up with a curriculum that is obviously a mismatch, don't hesitate to replace it with a new one!

5. How do you enroll?

Homeschooling is not something you enroll in; it's something you proclaim. I had to sign a declaration of intent to homeschool, which is how you start homeschooling in many states. When you decide to homeschool, the first step isn't enrolling; it's to check your state homeschool law.

Once you know what is required to start homeschooling in your state, register or sign your declaration of intent and you'll be officially on your way!

6. What if we have a family crisis while homeschooling?

Sometimes parents ask, "What if I start homeschooling and then we have a family crisis? What would we do?" While it is easy to withdraw from high school to start homeschooling and easy to get into college from high school, it can be difficult to return to public school once your child has started homeschooling. It's certainly not a life sentence to begin homeschooling high school though. If you find yourself in this situation, you have options.

When your child enters public high school after homeschooling, administrators may not know what to do with them unless they're at grade level. They will sometimes insist your child start with ninth grade even if you've already been homeschooling high school for three years.

Here are some options if you need to consider alternatives to independent homeschooling:

1. Instead of returning to high school, consider dual enrollment at the local community college. Many high school kids start at community college when they're 16 years old.

2. Seek some retroactive accreditation. Accrediting agencies will go over records you've kept as a homeschooler and provide an accredited transcript. I don't recommend this for most people because it's extremely expensive and usually unnecessary, but it can be a good back-up plan. Be aware, however, that some colleges view accrediting agencies as diploma mills.

3. Another option is to get a GED if it's necessary. Your child can officially graduate when they get a GED.

4. If the crisis is of your student's making, you may need to allow them to suffer the consequences and fail them.

If you return your child to public school, it rarely solves the problems that made you want to quit homeschooling, such as behavior problems, or drug and alcohol problems. Often these problems will remain or get increasingly worse. The only time I will suggest returning to public school is if it becomes impossible for you to continue home education with the safety of your children in mind.

7. What about the prom or other social functions?

Some people have fond memories of their high school prom and want their child to have the chance to experience an unforgettable evening, too. For others, remembering the prom brings back negative feelings or embarrassment about their own (or their date's) behavior. You might remember a lot of drama when you think back to your own prom. For teens today, it seems like prom is an even higher stakes affair with unrealistic expectations of luxuries, such as expensive dinners, limousines, and after parties. You should think twice before allowing your child to dip their toe into this world.

Prom is not always a positive event and it's not a necessary part of growing up. However, some homeschool groups have put together great homeschool proms. I once attended a homeschool prom held at a swing dance studio. My boys were not interested in the prom, but one of my sons organized an annual Jane Austen-style Pemberley Ball while he was in college. If you love organizing events, you could help your local homeschool group organize a prom or other social event.

Chapter 4

Requirements for Success

There are a few critical ingredients you need to homeschool independently with excellence. Here are some essentials.

Homeschool Requirements

1. Time. Homeschooling requires time. Some homeschoolers have one parent stay home to homeschool full time. It is possible, but challenging, to work and homeschool at the same time. Some parents work opposite shifts so one of them is always available at home to teach. Many homeschool parents work from home, and even take their child to work with them in some situations. It is possible to work alongside your child, or share the workload with another homeschooling parent. Single parents often pair up and take turns teaching each other's children. Supervision is especially required in the younger grades, but even teenagers can get into a lot of trouble without proper supervision.

2. Money. Homeschooling costs money, but there is no set dollar amount you have to spend. The national average spent on homeschool curriculum is about $600 per child per year. That's quite a deal since $600 doesn't even pay for a month of private school! Some homeschoolers spend much more and some spend much less. You can make homeschooling fit into your budget, even if you don't have much. There are many resources and an entire website devoted to homeschooling for free.

3. Love. This is the key requirement. You have to love your child and love spending time with them to homeschool. There is no substitute for the love you have for your child. The good news is that your feelings of love will increase as you spend more time with your child. Your child will even gain better social skills as they spend more time with your family, people who share your values, and people who know how to behave. Believe me, this type of socialization is far superior to being confined in a room full of misbehaving peers.

4. Effort. Homeschooling is not always easy and it does take the whole family's effort to accomplish. When I was homeschooling, I taught my children to get their chores done first, before homeschool work. That way, they participated in the care of the home to lighten my load. We all worked together as we were at home and schooling.

5. Patience. Homeschooling requires patience. However, it only requires a normal, parental amount of patience. Many people assume homeschool parents must have superhuman amounts of patience. I assure you, I certainly don't and neither do the other homeschoolers I know.

6. Ownership. Parents have to take ownership of the homeschooling process. This means you are in charge; you need to see things through. You don't have to be perfect all the time, though. Consider what it's like when you're an employee - you don't have to be perfect at your job, you just have to take ownership of your job and do what's required on a day-to-day basis. Take it one day at a time in your homeschool as well.

There are also things people often think are required, but are not.

NOT Required to Homeschool

1. High income. Families at all income levels homeschool their children. In fact, the average homeschool family's income is not higher than the national average.

2. Gifted children. Although homeschoolers do tend to have higher test scores than their public and private schooled peers, it's not because they are all gifted. Children perform better when they are taught at their level in every subject. Homeschooled kids are not passed on to the next grade level in math every year even if they're not ready. Homeschooling is a very effective method of education!

3. Perfect children. Your children don't have to be perfectly obedient to homeschool successfully. Seek reasonable compliance instead of perfection. As long as your child is reasonably compliant and obedient, you should have no trouble jumping into homeschooling.

4. Specific ages. Your child doesn't need to be a specific age to homeschool. I have a friend in Oregon whose child was in fourth grade when she first contacted me. She said she would homeschool but thought her child was too old; she contacted me again when her child was in seventh grade and told me again her child was too old to be homeschooled. She contacted me yet again when her daughter was in tenth grade. Her daughter ended up graduating high school with a diploma and post-traumatic stress disorder, requiring years of counseling. They tried public schools and private schools, and nothing was a good fit. She wishes she had started her homeschooling journey when her daughter was in fourth grade. You can start homeschooling for the first time in Kindergarten, in high school, or any time in between.

5. A specific method of homeschooling. There are many different methods of homeschooling. There is no perfect method and every homeschooler has their own favorite style. You are free to choose the one that matches your child perfectly, or you can choose a method and curriculum that is the perfect blend between your learning style and your child's learning style to make it more meaningful for both of you.

6. A college degree. Studies show that even if a homeschool parent does not have a college degree or high school diploma, their children perform equally well as children of parents who have a college degree. A college degree will not improve the outcome of your homeschooling, so homeschool without fear, regardless of your level of education!

7. A teaching degree. A teaching degree is not required, either. You are a real teacher when you homeschool. A teaching certificate will not make you a better home educator and it will not improve your results. In fact, a teaching degree can often be a burden the parent carries with them into homeschooling. Teachers spend years learning how to teach a group of 30 children and not much of that translates into teaching a few siblings. It's a different animal altogether.

Chapter 5

Problems with Dependence

One of the problems with modern homeschooling is there are so many resources available that it's hard to remember none of them are required. Some of these resources resemble public or private school resources and may not be a good fit for your children.

You do not have to be an expert to teach your child, not even for high school subjects. Try to be more of an encourager and coach so your children can become independent learners. You don't have to teach physics, you just have to teach your child how to learn it.

One of my clients from New Mexico told me she wants to cover the basics but feels pressure to be rigorous and thinks she is behind. Often homeschoolers feel that way when they're involved in large groups that resemble schools. If you homeschool independently, these feelings will likely go away.

Tutors and hired teachers can be useful or they can make your homeschool resemble a classroom and cause you to feel as if you cannot do it on your own. One homeschool mom I know of hired a tutor for every homeschool class; she didn't teach a single class on her own. If a tutor or teacher takes care of everything, you can start feeling insecure about teaching anything on your own.

That's one of the big problems with dependence: feeling insecure. You won't feel responsible for your child's successes, such as learning to read. You may feel inadequate and as if you always have to look to the teacher to make the decisions.

When you are dependent, you feel a loss of control over how best to teach your own, unique child. The teacher may use a curriculum or method that doesn't fit your child or their learning style. Teachers may even increase your workload, especially if they are part of an online school. They usually require additional paperwork from you, so it can end up being more of a hassle than homeschooling independently.

Parent Partnership Programs

Virtual schools and other private and government funded "parent partnership programs" will benefit financially when you feel afraid and incapable. Look carefully at the language of their advertisements. They're trying to convince you that you're inadequate in order to sell their program.

Advertisements for parent partnership programs often include mention of providing "real" teachers. They will brag about the expertise of their teachers, but in the homeschool you're the teacher and you're the one who loves your child.

You know what is in your child's best interests. The best advice for your child comes from you following your own heart, using your own expertise.

Don't be fooled; homeschooling parents are real teachers – the best possible teachers for their children. You can provide your children with all the skills they need to succeed in the world. As the parent, you are 100% qualified to teach your children - not because you are an expert in English, history, or economics, and not because you know how to grade an essay test perfectly. You are qualified because you are your children's parent; you're the one who knows them and loves them best.

Advertisements claim to have a "great student-teacher ratio" or "one-to-one student-teacher interaction." Remember that homeschoolers have the same one-to-one student-teacher ratio, but we also have the advantage of knowing our children better than anyone else. When we retain our homeschool independence, we can choose our own curriculum.

Advertisements for parent partnership programs sometimes claim that each child's curriculum package is individualized. However, when you look them over carefully, they only offer certain textbooks, workbooks, and school-at-home programs that won't be a good fit for every child. Choices may not include the ones you need to meet your child's needs. They may claim to use an approved curriculum, but they approve the curriculum, not you; it's not chosen based on what is the best fit for your children and their learning styles.

Parent partnership programs claim they provide real high school diplomas. When you homeschool independently, YOU provide the real homeschool diploma. My children's high school diplomas were real enough to earn college admission and full-tuition scholarships. These programs boast about accredited transcripts, but colleges are used to seeing transcripts from unaccredited public and private schools, as well as homeschoolers.

Are you being sucked into an advertisement because it claims that courses range from vocational to advanced placement? You can also offer a range of classes while homeschooling independently. You can provide advanced courses and remedial courses. You are not limited in your curriculum options and can provide any class your child needs at any level, no matter how strange or unusual your child's interests.

In addition to offering online courses, these parent partnership programs will also offer to do all your record keeping, for a hefty fee. They offer record keeping options for individual or co-op courses, but homeschoolers have options that go far beyond. You can include any educational experience on your own, official homeschool transcript. You can include a public school calculus class, band, a co-op class, distance learning, and community college. You can include what you did at home, the art class your child took, and their swim team experiences; the options are unlimited.

Look over the tuition costs of these programs carefully. Perhaps a program claims tuition is only $195 for the first student, but this may not include the curriculum or all the record keeping. These experiences can be much more expensive than you think, easily adding up to thousands of dollars. This is expensive, since the average homeschooler spends only about $600 per student per year!

Look closely at the messages these programs communicate. Weigh the pros and cons and consider carefully before choosing. You don't have to be afraid of homeschooling independently – there's no reason for concern. Don't make a decision based on fear because of advertisements designed to play on them.

Parent partnership programs are often tied to the federal government. Follow the money because these programs benefit financially when you feel incapable and afraid. They may claim to love homeschoolers and may initially say they will not control your homeschool, but they can and often will.

Government money means government control. When you take government money, it means they can control your homeschool. They can force you to comply with the common core even if you don't like it, to use a program that does not follow your beliefs, and control your curriculum. Because they're tied to the public schools, every time the public school rules change, their program will change with it.

These programs require your child to be evaluated by a certified teacher, sometimes for a certain number of hours, or to submit work for grading. If you are paying them to compile your records while homeschooling independently, they may not approve of your curriculum. They may not allow you to teach from your own worldview, use a religious curriculum, or include any religious instruction in your homeschool day. If you are a believer, how do you separate your beliefs from the information you teach your children each day?

The Problems of Certified Teachers

Many homeschoolers who are certified teachers (with a public or private school background) contact me for support. Twenty to thirty percent of my Gold Care Club members are certified teachers who feel insecure and constrained. They know in their minds that homeschooling allows flexibility, but their college degree and classroom experience is screaming out for a highly structured regimen that doesn't fit, so they struggle to break free of the shackles. They may use a structured curriculum, but still feel insecure and reach out.

I am a registered nurse and because of my training, I know too much about diseases. Teachers attend college for years and know too much about what could go wrong in classrooms, so they have more difficulty seeing the forest for the trees. Homeschooling is not about the parent's education, it is about the parent's love and commitment.

As with parenting, there are insecurities that come with teaching and you aren't immune. Teachers feel insecure, too. There are many right ways to parent and there are many right ways to homeschool high school. Parenting is often difficult and the answers to parenting dilemmas never come easily. Homeschooling is similar; dilemmas come up, and homeschooling is not always easy, but it's certainly no more difficult than parenting.

Modeling Behavior

Children will imitate others. When a young child spouts off about a political issue, you might suspect that child learned this point of view from a schoolteacher. When homeschooling, your child will start to internalize conversations around your dining table and will start to imitate your behaviors. You want to model healthy behaviors instead of destructive behaviors. Ensure they encounter people who live out their lives with honor and integrity. Don't assume that because someone has an advanced degree and a teaching certificate they are an admirable role model. When you are the teacher, you know the quality of the teacher and the quality of conversations your child will absorb.

Homeschooling independently provides a real, quality education but the parents are responsible instead of a school. It can work within your own schedule and is completely flexible. If you work days and want to homeschool from 3 PM until 9 PM, you can.

Homeschooling creates independent learners, not spoon-fed receptacles of knowledge. You don't stand up in front of a classroom, lecturing and pouring knowledge into your child. Instead, you encourage your child to learn what they don't already know and learn how to learn it on their own.

College officials complain to me that public school kids enter college unprepared because they don't have the ability to learn. They are so used to sitting in a classroom being lectured that they don't know how to pursue knowledge on their own. As homeschoolers, we can do better because we have to; our children have to learn on their own since we may not know anything on advanced topics such as physics and Latin. When we create independent learners, we also become more successful as educators.

Old-fashioned vs. Modern Homeschooling

Old-fashioned homeschooling used to be the only way, with parents most often homeschooling on their own. In the early days, you couldn't even buy homeschool curriculum, just hand-me-down curriculum from private schools. Homeschool curriculum simply didn't exist. Parents were fully responsible for their children's education, with no accreditation programs, parent partnership programs, or alt-ed programs.

If you could travel back in time, you'd discover the typical homeschool consisted of mom, some kids, books, a dog, paper, and pencils, with no computers to be found. Old-fashioned homeschooling included co-ops that were simply small groups of parents (usually three or four friends) who gathered to share the teaching burden or do fun experiments together.

Homeschooling has changed. In decades past, homeschooling was always independent. Modern homeschooling has become more dependent on others and can resemble public or private schools. It may include formal online classes. There may be a physical schoolroom and a standardized curriculum. Homeschooling today often includes ubiquitous use of technology or homeschool co-ops with hundreds of kids, and teachers you don't know. Modern homeschooling includes abundant resources that are not required and can easily ensnare parents.

Homeschool Co-ops

Another way to be dependent is to homeschool using co-ops exclusively. Homeschool co-ops are popular, but they may not fit your family or your schedule, and may not support your educational goals or your child's needs. You may want to teach biology this year and all the co-op offers is chemistry. Some co-op programs are extremely rigorous, fitting only gifted children, yet they may tell you they fit all children.

There are some pros to working with a co-op. You can share responsibilities with other homeschoolers as well as expenses. You can all hire a chemistry tutor or purchase microscopes together. Co-ops can also increase socializing, but this can end up being negative. When you group teens together, their quality of socialization is not as good as when teens are mixed with parents.

Another negative is burnout, which I see often in my consulting work. When a parent tells me they're stressed out, struggling to keep up, and their child is failing, it often indicates they are involved in a dependent program (usually a homeschool co-op). These homeschoolers are using co-ops for core classes. In an effort to provide the right homeschool classes, they join co-op classes, feeling as if the masses must be homeschooling correctly. Instead, the co-op provides an assembly line production of lessons and children can become frustrated if they can't keep up, or bored if they're too far ahead.

One of my clients had a child involved in a co-op for almost all of his core classes. As much as he loved being with his friends, the classical education style curriculum didn't match his kinesthetic learning style. He needed to learn by doing and not by reading a bunch of books.

As I've mentioned, in years past a homeschool co-op was simply three or four moms coming together once a week to share a science experiment, an art project, or a unit study together. When older moms reminisce about co-ops, you'll notice they don't mention tests or classrooms; they don't remember concerns about childcare, mandatory babysitting for parents not in the classroom, or negative socialization. They do remember time spent bonding with a small group of students and parents who became close friends. There were no mega co-ops with a thousand students. Today, these huge co-ops often replace homeschool support groups, casual park days, or play arrangements.

It's important to look at the class size when you deal with any out-of-the-home situation. Independent homeschooling, of course, has a small class size with excellent student-teacher ratio and each lesson can be tailored to the individual. Programs and co-ops have much larger class sizes, tailored to the median (the 20% of kids in the middle academically). The result is children who face the same problems they would encounter in public and private schools.

Chapter 6

Systemic Educational Problems

The public education system forces children to behave in a way that minimizes classroom disruption. Children move along grade levels in an assembly line fashion. School is designed for progression from one stage to the next, instead of caring for the individual and their education. Getting along is the primary civic virtue.

Don't get me wrong, most teachers do care for their students. Care, however, is a lousy substitute for love. From a homeschooling perspective, the care of a teacher supervising students is not a quality substitute for the love of a parent. Children learn more and respond best to those who know and love them. Kids deserve the love and commitment of their parents when it comes to education. They deserve more than just the care of the state.

Children's innate hunger to learn can be suppressed by systemic neglect. If children are constantly placed in a setting where work is over their head, or incredibly boring, they can lose the hunger to learn. As much as you want public schools to provide a high quality education, they are not going to improve quickly enough to benefit your children. Systemic change will take much longer. Worse yet, given current trends, parents can't be sure the changes will be going in the right direction. Homeschooling provides an education perfectly suited for your student's needs. Parents can take ownership of their child's education.

Societal Change

Society changes all the time for good and for ill. It's easy to get overwhelmed with the pace of change and with some of the negativity. The steady erosion of character qualities and behavior is evident in public schools. Both increase the uneasiness and fear students may feel. When you homeschool, you can educate your children in a way that protects and nurtures them so they can learn without fear. Children always learn best when they are not afraid.

We want our children to use their unique, God-given gifts to get an education perfectly suited to their needs. No matter what innate skills children begin with, from the most gifted to the most academically challenged, they all have something meaningful to bring to college or career by the time they graduate high school. We want to take ownership of our children's education to ensure it's the best possible.

Some parent begin homeschooling because public school has failed their child, or they have fallen behind in some way. Failing grades on a public or private high school transcript are part of the dreaded "permanent record." Homeschool parents still have some options, however. Before high school begins, nothing is permanent. It doesn't matter if they fail eighth grade or earn F's in seventh grade. Independent homeschool parents can begin high school at exactly the ability level of their child, and avoid failure altogether. But if a child was in public or private high school and fail, what can you do? Homeschool parents can have the child repeat the class as a homeschooler. Perhaps they take Algebra 1 over again, so they can learn it well, understanding it thoroughly, and replace the failed grade.

In that situation, it will help to provide some outside documentation proving the child learned the material, even though the prior school's transcript indicated the first failure. Consider having your child take an SAT Subject Test to prove they learned the subject. Sometimes I recommend people explain failing grades in a cover letter to colleges with each application package. You can decide to have your child repeat the class and teach it yourself, in a way that is more meaningful for your child. You can give a grade based on what the student knows, how hard they worked, or extra credit.

The programs your child has been involved with may not provide a transcript. If your child participated in one of these programs and earned a failing grade, these are not part of the permanent record. Parents can use outside classes for supplements, and grades provided are a serving suggestion, rather than a requirement. When an outside program does not give a transcript, parents do not need to do anything about it other than keep on educating their children. Parents can choose to have a child repeat the class, or drop the class, or use the outside class for a portion of the overall grade, rather than the entire grade.

When you homeschool independently, you can prevent your child from failing. It's easy to find a math assessment test to determine your child's level, but there is no standard grade level for many other subjects – it's all about ability level. Give your child the opportunity to learn at their ability level in every subject, every year. Teach to a level of mastery so your child is always learning something. Challenging your student without overwhelming them is the goal. If children do not feel overwhelmed, they can succeed.

Chapter 7

First Steps Toward Independence

When you homeschool independently, you can choose the perfect fit curriculum or teach any elective under the sun; the world is your oyster. When you tie yourself to a school system or alternative education program, you lose all control. Homeschooling independently allows you to provide a superior education that's a perfect fit for your children.

Independent homeschooling is flexible, individualized, supportive, and official. Independent homeschooling is not flexible within boundaries, individualized within certain curriculum choices, or supportive as long as the rules are followed. The only requirement for independent homeschooling is to obey state law.

Know the Law and Seek Support

The first step towards independence is to know your state homeschool law. It is not the same as your public school law, so do not search for state graduation requirements; they only tell you what public high school kids need to do. Instead, read your state homeschool law. Homeschooling is legal in every state in the United States.

It is important to follow your state law, because it's the law, but also so you have a record of the letters of intent to homeschool. Parents in certain states have found their children ineligible for college scholarships because they neglected to sign their declaration of intent.

Contact your state homeschool group and get to know some local homeschoolers. Speak to a veteran homeschooler and learn how to get started in your state. Many churches also have homeschool support groups.

Locate support for you and friendships for your child, trying to separate the social opportunities from the academics. Your child won't lose all their friends from any previous school. You can encourage them to keep healthy friendships.

Getting Started

If your child has been in a public or private school setting and you've decided to homeschool them, consider spending some time deschooling first. Sometimes kids are so overwhelmed by what happened to them in school that they may be experiencing a bit of post-traumatic stress. Your child may need to take a break for one or more months to enjoy field trips and spend time deschooling so they can regain the love of learning. You can start by reading the book, *Deschooling Gently: A Step by Step Guide to Fearless Homeschooling*. While your child is deschooling, you can research homeschooling; make sure you spend enough time to understand how homeschooling works and what kinds of homeschool curriculum are available so you can make good decisions.

You want to start homeschooling when you are called – don't wait to do it. If you need a gentle start, then at the beginning just focus on some reading and writing. Determine your interim plan: reading, writing, and journal. All you need to do is go to the library, read together, and have your child write by keeping a journal, writing to Grandma, or starting a blog.

If your child is motivated, willing, and you want to get right into homeschooling, consider picking up a grade-level workbook from the dollar store or an SAT or ACT preparation book for high school age. Your child can use it to practice their reading, writing, and math each day. If you have eager learners, give them what they want and start quickly by diving in. You can modify your plan later on. Children are often little sponges wanting to soak it all up.

Keep calm and move forward. Mark the new beginning by having a celebration. Tell your kids, "First day of homeschool! We made it! Let's celebrate!" It can help get your homeschool off in the right direction.

Get to Know Your Child

Spend some time getting to know your child. I know that may sound funny, but if they have been in public school awhile, you may not have noticed how their personality, likes, and dislikes have changed. Spend time together, even if you're simply working together. There's no substitute for time. Spending time together can improve your teenager's behavior and develop family closeness. It can even improve your child's manners as your child becomes attached to you instead of to other children.

Spend some time getting to know your child's learning style. Is your child primarily an auditory, visual, or kinesthetic learner? Often an auditory learner will say, "I hear you." A visual learner will say, "I see what you mean" or "Let me see that." A kinesthetic learner will say, "Feel this, mom" or "Let me do it." Research learning styles and try to figure out the best way to get knowledge into your child in a meaningful way.

Homeschool Methods

Consider the different homeschool methods. There are so many options. You can use a literature-based method and curriculum as I did (since my kids love reading). There is also the classical method, the Charlotte Mason method (using living books), hands-on or child-led learning with unit studies, delight directed learning, or unschooling, to name a few. Some homeschooling methods are based on worldview, either faith-based or secular.

Another method is school-at-home, which might be an option for you, especially if you're feeling overwhelmed. However, if your child has left a formal school system for any reason, the chances are slim that a school-at-home curriculum will be a good fit.

Parent as Guidance Counselor

When homeschooling independently, you can learn how to be the best guidance counselor for your child and excel in your job. The parent creates a transcript and high school diploma. The high school diploma will be unaccredited, but still official.

Part of your job as guidance counselor is to plan classes. First, determine what classes they need; think about it in terms of changing school districts. If your child moved from Montana to Colorado and changed schools, their previous school experience doesn't completely go away; it's taken into consideration as they move into the new school district.

Chapter 8

Plan Classes and Choose Resources

Determine what you need. Consider what your child has already completed. If your child has already attended school, you don't want to start from the beginning; you want to collect what your child has previously learned. Get a copy of your child's public or private school transcript and list classes already taken. Then try to figure out what is missing and what you need to cover next. If your child wasn't doing well in certain classes, you might want to consider tests to determine your child's ability, particularly in math. Don't introduce your child to advanced math when they're not ready for pre-algebra work. Determine if you will handle any failed classes from previous school experience, by repeating them or testing for current ability.

Choosing a Curriculum

When choosing a curriculum, take into consideration your strengths, weaknesses, and abilities. How organized are you? Should you buy a homeschool curriculum that has built-in organization? Consider your child's strengths, weaknesses, and learning style as well.

Choose a curriculum that's intended for homeschoolers, because they assume the parent knows nothing about the subject and that the child is going to learn the subject side-by-side with you. Learn your children's preferences and listen to their input about curriculum choices. To help you choose homeschool resources, I recommend buying the book, *102 Top Picks for Homeschool Curriculum* by Cathy Duffy, and reading her thorough curriculum reviews.

Life is filled with seasons. In some seasons, you may depend on a more structured curriculum. Other seasons may find you more capable and eager to choose resources confidently, and mix and match. If the workbook format or unschooling fits into the current season of your life, then give yourself the freedom to use that method.

You can use each curriculum as written and strictly adhere to it. You can also modify, adapt, and adjust the curriculum for a better fit. Feel free to mix and match and choose different curriculum for each subject (this is often referred to as the eclectic method). Homeschoolers have the freedom to learn in many different ways over their years of homeschooling. Get more tips for choosing curriculum in my book, *Homeschool Curriculum That's Effective and Fun*. You can find all of my books on my Amazon author's page:

amazon.com/author/leebinz

You can create your own curriculum by simply collecting library resources and documenting the resources used throughout the year.

How to Develop Your Own Class

1. Decide what you want to teach.
2. Search for resources that fit. For example, if you decide to teach economics then start searching for homeschool economics curriculum.
3. Choose ready-made curriculum or a set amount of time each day.
4. Dig deeply or cover broadly. Dig deeply sometimes to foster the love of learning or to kindle a passionate interest in the topic. Covering broadly may give your child an appreciation of the topic and suggest related areas they may want to study next.
5. To cover a subject, choose a guideline to follow. For history, it could be a world history book or a timeline to make sure you cover what you intend.
6. Locate a virtual outline for the topics. There are many available online you can reference.

Think about how much time you want to spend on each subject each day. If you're pulling each class together yourself, remember that a high school credit equals about an hour per day of work. As long as you do enough to keep your child busy for an hour a day, you'll be able to call it American History class, knowing it's a full credit.

If you want to dig deeply, it's a good idea to try to complete core classes one year at a time. You can work on American history for a year and world history for a year. That will make creating your homeschool transcript a little easier. I started with Sonlight curriculum because I felt it helped me through the process of mixing and matching, giving me the guidance and organization I needed to work through the whole school year with momentum and finish each course.

If you look through a textbook, such as a Bob Jones history text, it will tell you what topics to cover, how fast to move through them, and how to move through the topics in order to avoid getting stuck. You can use the textbook as a guideline and supplement the class with other resources, or use the textbook as a list of ideas for your own course. Compile videos from The Great Courses to cover each of the time periods. Borrow some biographies from the library. Pick up an atlas from the dollar store. Use some hands-on ideas you can find online. You can cover American history in one year and make it your own by developing your own class using an outline.

A friend of mine wanted to do a study on musicals with her 11th grader. A pre-made study would be difficult to find. Have your child work for one hour per day studying musicals. You could call it, "Musical Theater" and award a fine arts credit. Alternatively, you could wrap the study of musical theater into an all-encompassing class involving history, English, and art. As long as you work at the history part of it for one hour a day, the English for one hour a day, and the art for one hour a day, you could wrap your whole school day around one theme that appeals to your child and award credit for each class.

Schools don't teach everything perfectly or cover every event in history. It's often quite shocking what public schools don't teach. If you miss something small in any of your classes, don't worry about it too much. You can also choose to fill it in if you want to. For example, if you didn't quite get to cover the Civil War as deeply as you wanted, you might watch and discuss the Ken Burns' series, *The Civil War*.

Chapter 9

Avoid Fads and Pitfalls

You don't need to imitate the public school system. New homeschoolers often have a hard time realizing this at first. You do not need desks, blackboards, a bell signaling class is in session, or a flag in the corner. You don't need to include the pledge of allegiance, recess, or fill-in-the-bubble tests.

You can avoid public school norms, fads and pitfalls. Also make sure you don't repeat public school failures. Don't sign up for a school program or curriculum if the school has previously failed your child. Also avoid online schools, classrooms, or DVDs with classroom settings if your child has not done well in those settings while in public or private school. In that case, avoid textbooks or workbooks and aim for a more natural approach to learning as you adapt to homeschooling and help your child regain the love of learning.

Avoid the public school system mentality of grade level thinking. There isn't a set grade level for English, art, or music. Everybody has a different ability level. Take that mindset with you as you delve into other subjects as well. Make homeschool decisions based on your child's ability level in each subject instead. It is common to hear homeschoolers or parents talk about how their child is in 7th grade math, 10th grade English and 6th grade science.

You can keep children challenged but not overwhelmed in each class. This means they learn something new, and should be capable of success. Don't give them algebra 1 level work before they understand mathematics completely. A true sign of success is when you're able to mix and match levels from different subjects. Strive for mastery, not perfection. Nobody is perfect – not me, not you, and not your child.

My children were quite bright and academically advanced in public school, which was a large part of why we started homeschooling. When we began homeschooling, they were shocked because it was the first time they had to learn something they didn't already know! There were some tears. They had no idea school was for learning; they thought school was merely for reciting information you already knew.

The biggest fad in homeschooling today is dual enrolment. Dual enrolment is a student taking community college classes while in high school and earning high school and college credit at the same time. Beware, because community college can be a rated-R environment; it's not appropriate for all homeschooled children. Dual enrolment may be helpful when children are academically ahead, but it probably won't be helpful when children are academically behind.

Curriculum fads change over time. Homeschool methods also go in and out of style. In some years, un-schooling is IN and it seems like everybody is doing it. You might feel that if you're not unschooling, then you're not successful. In recent years, there has been a powerful move towards classical education. Curriculum also takes turns being in style. Fellow homeschoolers will say you have to use a specific curriculum because it's considered the best right now.

Beware of peer pressure from well-meaning parents; their advice may not fit. Stand firm and don't follow the crowd. Instead, use what works for your family and your child. Adults are susceptible to peer pressure just as our children are. Be a good example, especially for your teens.

Chapter 10

How to Teach the Hard Stuff

Subjects such as physics and calculus can be a bit intimidating. Purchase homeschool curriculum that fits your child. Don't teach what you don't know – instead, facilitate learning as a project manager. Focus on helping your child to learn independently as much as possible; it's the goal.

My husband is an engineering manager at Boeing. He doesn't build the planes; as the project manager, he's in-charge of the people who build the planes. You can be a project manager, too. You don't have to "build the plane" yourself; you have to make sure it is built.

Allow children to do the work and then use the answer key so they can check it. Provide video tutorials, hands-on learning, and supplements for them. This way, your teenagers will start to learn independently. Success in school and life depends on knowing how to learn independently.

If you were in a job or situation you weren't familiar with, you would learn how to do the task; that's what successful adults do. They know how to learn independently.

Be conscientious and learn on purpose every day. Don't worry about how far you get through your curriculum plan, especially in the beginning. It's hard to judge how much your children can accomplish in one day, and whether you're biting off more than you can chew. As long as you learn on purpose every day, consider yourself successful.

A big key to success is to have a daily morning meeting. Sit down with your child every day (I preferred mornings). Explain what you want your child to do, go over their assignments, and review yesterday's work.

Another key to success is to put your weakest areas first. If your child is weak in math, then get that subject over with first each day. It's the one subject you make sure they complete. This way, you won't put it off until the year's over and you realize you've avoided the subject all year! You may not always get everything done, but commit to always getting your child's weakest subject area done.

Don't fight your child over their interests and passions. You can include natural learning on your child's homeschool transcript. Even if that's playing their electric guitar or riding their skateboard, it counts as delight directed learning, which can be included as their music class or P.E. class.

When your children do activities for fun, you don't have to turn them into schoolwork. Do not create a fill-in-the-bubble test for voluntary P.E. or music work. Simply count delight directed learning on the high school transcript.

Keep in mind the rule of thumb for awarding credit:

> One credit = 120-180 hours, or about 1 hour a day
> Half credit = 60-90 hours, or about ½ hour per day

No tests are required; instead, you can evaluate holistically. Don't beat the love of learning out of the subject. If you know your child plays the guitar for more than an hour a day, give them one credit of music. You can include natural writing assignments if you want to. It might be a good idea to assign an essay about what they like.

A Special Note about Video Games and Other Time-Wasters

The number one complaint I hear from parents is that their kids are obsessed with playing video games (usually online). While I am wary of children spending too much time on the computer for any reason, I am also aware that this area of passionate interest can sometimes lead to fruitful areas of learning. Gamers may decide they want to learn the coding behind the games. The artistically minded might decide to learn visual design or how to illustrate. Playing the games themselves should be carefully monitored by parents, but also be aware of what it can teach you about your student. Perhaps it is pointing to a related field of study that might captivate them and push them on to new areas of study.

A great example of how one interest can lead to another was my eldest son, who was fully engrossed in chess as a teen. He spent hours upon hours each day studying and playing. I must admit that I thought it was a total waste of time. Chess is like playing Monopoly, right? Doesn't everyone know that?

Apparently, I was wrong, and eventually had to repent from every harsh judgement I had made about my son and his obsession with chess. I learned of my error when we visited his first choice college after he gained admission and was considering his major. My son asked one of the professors, "What is the toughest major you have?" When the professor answered, "Electrical Engineering," that was all my son needed to make his ultimate choice.

I was shocked. He had never expressed interest in engineering as a career choice. All he had wanted to do was play chess. Apparently, chess taught him several key things about himself:

- He liked to think deeply
- He enjoyed figuring out complex problems
- He was drawn to long-term strategic thought
- He loved doing hard things.

That sounds like the makings of a great engineer to me! The lesson here is to pay attention to anything your child shows passionate interest in, whether or not you think it is a total waste of time. It may not be their life direction, but it may be a signpost pointing to something greater beyond the next rise.

Chapter 11

Homeschooling is Your Job!

Homeschooling independently declares the parent responsible for their child's education. You are responsible for providing a quality high school education and can't get away from that responsibility.

Parents are financially and emotionally motivated to create independent young adults. We are financially motivated because we want to ensure we don't have to support our grown children for the next 50 years; we eventually want them to grow up and become self-supporting. We are emotionally motivated because we want them to succeed as adults and become emotionally independent.

You cannot delegate your entire responsibility, but you can delegate small jobs or certain courses such as math or economics. Beware of delegating by enrolling in a program and giving up your independence.

Programs, schools, and academies require work at a certain pace or on a certain schedule, much like an assembly line. They don't know your children and may simply give you age-based curriculum. They require submitted work, and may determine grades without your input and without knowing what your children are capable of or how much they worked.

One of the most frustrating moments I had in public school was when they gave my child an A for writing one paragraph about his dog, "My dog is white and fluffy..." At home he was penning five pages of creative writing simply for fun. It's frustrating when somebody gives grades without knowing what your child is capable of or how hard they're working.

You can provide a real, quality education better than public schools or any homeschooling "program" can provide. No program can fit your child as perfectly as independent homeschooling.

Take your job seriously. This is your chosen vocation, so you need to consider continuing education. Learn about how to homeschool all the way through high school. Invest in classes and attend homeschool conventions; learn more about homeschooling every year. Get the support you need to do the job well. You don't have to be a member of a formal support group, but make sure to develop friendships with other homeschoolers, especially the veteran ones.

If you would like to lean on me for additional support through high school, consider joining my **Gold Care Club**. In addition to training, tools, and templates, club members are entitled to a 20 minute, personal email or phone consultation each week to get questions answered and boost confidence.

Learn more about the Gold Care Club here:

www.TheHomeScholar.com/Gold-Care.php

Conclusion

Taking Charge

Independent homeschooling is all about taking charge. Seize the reins and do not delegate your responsibility. Don't make your homeschooling decision based on fear. Independent homeschooling is individualized, flexible, supportive, and official. Homeschool parents can provide the opportunities their children need.

Homeschooling is a continuum, with various levels of independence. Sometimes you will find it important to use a standard curriculum or school-at-home curriculum. At other times, you will want to take the complete opposite approach. Parents can choose the curriculum that meets their child's learning style, their own teaching style, and the abilities and interests of their student. You can make different choices each year.

Once you have taken control, notify your family and friends. Expect to have to explain homeschooling, especially to grandparents. Homeschooling may be unfamiliar to some of your family members. Tell your extended family about your decision. You don't need your family's permission – you are your child's parent.

You do have a safety net - your spouse, supportive friends and family, and the local homeschool community. You have all of the skills you need to find resources when you need them. You can make all the decisions necessary to provide a quality education.

My job as a homeschool consultant is to encourage parents to homeschool independently through high school. If you need support or have questions, I specialize in helping parents who homeschool using any method. I do not judge anyone for using certain homeschool programs. My mission is to nudge parents gently toward homeschooling independently by giving them the tools and knowledge to feel confident. I believe parents are the best at making the right decisions for their children.

For more reading on homeschooling independently, check out these articles on my website,

www.TheHomeScholar.com

- **Delight directed learning information:** *Maximize the Fun Factor* and *Delight Directed Learning*
- **Homeschool Co-op Fad:** *Cooped Up in a Co-op?*
- **Dual Enrollment Fad:** *Facing the Community College Fad*
- **Alternative Education Fad:** *Parent Partnership Problems "Love with Some Strings Attached"*

Afterword

Who is Lee Binz and What Can She Do for Me?

Number one best-selling homeschool author, Lee Binz is The HomeScholar. Her mission is "helping parents homeschool high school." Lee and her husband Matt homeschooled their two boys, Kevin and Alex, from elementary through high school.

Upon graduation, both boys received four-year, full tuition scholarships from their first choice university. This enables Lee to pursue her dream job - helping parents homeschool their children through high school.

On The HomeScholar website, you will find great products for creating homeschool transcripts and comprehensive records to help you amaze and impress colleges.

Find out why Andrew Pudewa, Founder of the Institute for Excellence in Writing says, "Lee Binz knows how to navigate this often confusing and frustrating labyrinth better than anyone."

You can find Lee online at:

www.TheHomeScholar.com

If this book has been helpful, could you please take a minute to write us a quick review on Amazon?

Thank you!

Testimonials

Wisdom to Help a Frazzled Homeschool Mom

"I want to thank you for all that you have done for me in my homeschool-mom journey. I've been a **Gold Care Club** member for a long time and it has been invaluable to me. Many people in my life would question how in the world a homeschooler could get into college. Your services, webinars and conferences as a Gold Care Club member helped me gain the confidence I needed.

When college application time came, I freaked out! You were the voice of reason, and you guided me towards your Transcript Pajama Party. My son wrote his essays, and the applications were submitted. He didn't get into every school he applied to, but he got acceptance letters! And SCHOLARSHIP offers!!

So, thank you Lee! I know The HomeScholar is your business, but honestly, it's like a ministry as well. You have such a gift and such wisdom to help a frazzled homeschool mom gain the confidence she needs to homeschool high school. As I write this email, I have another high schooler that I am homeschooling. I thought I would have it all together by now, but I don't! I can't wait until I can get my membership going again. I need you Lee!!"

~ Jen in PA

Following Advice for 3 Years = College Admission & Scholarships

"I have been following your advice for 3 years now! Last year I leaped into the

Gold Care Club with the purchase of the **Comprehensive Record Solution**. I am so thankful for your willingness to mentor the homeschool community. My family has just gone through the college application process for the first time. Thanks to you, I felt very aware of what to expect, and confident in our coursework, preparation and transcript.

We chose to send a full package, with a cover letter, school profile, table of contents, transcript and course descriptions to each college our daughter applied to, though none required anything other than the transcript. Her top three college choices have already sent acceptance letters with initial scholarship offers based on GPA and test scores. As a homeschooling mother, teacher, tutor and guidance counselor, I truly appreciate all you do!"

~ Kathy in NE

For more information about my **Comprehensive Record Solution** and **Gold Care Club**, go to:

www.ComprehensiveRecordSolution.com
and
www.TheHomeScholar.com/Gold-Care.php

Also From The HomeScholar...

- The HomeScholar Guide to College Admission and Scholarships: Homeschool Secrets to Getting Ready, Getting In and Getting Paid (Book and Kindle Book)
- Setting the Records Straight - How to Craft Homeschool Transcripts and Course Descriptions for College Admission and Scholarships (Book and Kindle Book)
- Total Transcript Solution (Online Training, Tools and Templates)
- Comprehensive Record Solution (Online Training, Tools and Templates)

- Gold Care Club (Comprehensive Online Support and Training)
- Preparing to Homeschool High School (DVD)
- Finding a College (DVD)
- The Easy Truth About Homeschool Transcripts (Kindle Book)
- Parent Training A la Carte (Online Training)
- Homeschool "Convention at Home" Kit (Book, DVDs and Audios)

The HomeScholar "Coffee Break Books" Released or Coming Soon on Kindle and Paperback:

- Delight Directed Learning: Guiding Your Homeschooler Toward Passionate Learning
- Creating Transcripts for Your Unique Child: Help Your Homeschool Graduate Stand Out from the Crowd
- Beyond Academics: Preparation for College and for Life
- Planning High School Courses: Charting the Course Toward High School Graduation
- Graduate Your Homeschooler in Style: Make Your Homeschool Graduation Memorable

- Keys to High School Success: Get Your Homeschool High School Started Right!
- Getting the Most Out of Your Homeschool This Summer: Learning just for the Fun of it!
- Finding a College: A Homeschooler's Guide to Finding a Perfect Fit
- College Scholarships for High School Credit: Learn and Earn With This Two-for-One Strategy!
- College Admission Policies Demystified: Understanding Homeschool Requirements for Getting In
- A Higher Calling: Homeschooling High School for Harried Husbands (by Matt Binz, Mr. HomeScholar)
- Gifted Education Strategies for Every Child: Homeschool Secrets for Success
- College Application Essays: A Primer for Parents
- Creating Homeschool Balance: Find Harmony Between Type A and Type Zzz...
- Homeschooling the Holidays: Sanity Saving Strategies and Gift Giving Ideas
- Your Goals this Year: A Year by Year Guide to Homeschooling High School

- Making the Grades: A Grouch-Free Guide to Homeschool Grading
- High School Testing: Knowledge That Saves Money
- Getting the BIG Scholarships: Learn Expert Secrets for Winning College Cash!
- Easy English for Simple Homeschooling: How to Teach, Assess and Document High School English
- Scheduling - The Secret to Homeschool Sanity: Plan You Way Back to Mental Health
- Junior Year is the Key to High School Success: How to Unlock the Gate to Graduation and Beyond
- Upper Echelon Education: How to Gain Admission to Elite Universities
- How to Homeschool College: Save Time, Reduce Stress and Eliminate Debt
- Homeschool Curriculum That's Effective and Fun: Avoid the Crummy Curriculum Hall of Shame!
- Comprehensive Homeschool Records: Put Your Best Foot Forward to Win College Admission and Scholarships
- Options After High School: Steps to Success for College or Career

- How to Homeschool 9th and 10th Grade: Simple Steps for Starting Strong!
- Senior Year Step-by-Step: Simple Instructions for Busy Homeschool Parents
- High School Math The Easy Way: Simple Strategies for Homeschool Parents In Over Their Heads

Would you like to be notified when we offer one of our *Coffee Break Books* for FREE during our Kindle promotion days? If so, leave your name and email at the link below and we will send you a reminder.

http://www.TheHomeScholar.com/freekindlebook.php

Visit my Amazon Author Page!

amazon.com/author/leebinz

Made in the USA
Lexington, KY
19 May 2017